Cars go fast.

Cars go slow.

Start the engine.

Here we go!

See those old cars.

See those new cars.

See that big car.

See that small car.

See that fire truck.

See that garbage truck.

See that dump truck.

See that oil truck.

See that white truck.

See it's stopping.

It has ice cream!

It has topping.
Yum-yum!